"*A Better Way to Fall* offers the reader fifteen poems full of cruel irony and beautiful precision, Greek mythology mixed with contemporary mass media, global vision and neighborhood close-up. These poems of our moment presented in an all-of-a-piece orchestration are readily understandable and profoundly meaningful. They tell a reader that an instant in the sun might be worth the fall. They warn a reader that too often innocence does not lead to experience but instead self-induced ignorance ends in cliché: events, as well as sounds, repeat. Falling may be necessary, these poems say, if we plan — someday — to rise or, at least, 'navigate escape.'"

— Dennis Barone

A BETTER WAY TO FALL

POEMS BY
DAVID O'CONNELL

THE PROVIDENCE ATHENAEUM

Providence, Rhode Island

ISBN 0-922558-72-8

Published in cooperation with The Poet's Press

A Better Way to Fall takes its title from the song "Bukowski"
    by Modest Mouse
The Edith Hamilton quotation is from *Mythology: Timeless Tales
    of Gods and Heroes* (New York: Penguin, 1940)
The F. Scott Fitzgerald quotation is from *The Great Gatsby*
    (New York: Simon & Schuster, 1925)

Cover Art: *Untitled* by Peter Campbell
(petercampbellfineart.com)

This chapbook is published by the Providence Athenaeum as
part of the Philbrick Poetry Project, established in 1998 to
honor the memory of Charles and Deborah Philbrick. The
Philbrick Poetry Project honors an outstanding, emerging New
England poet who has not yet published a book. Dennis Barone
selected *A Better Way to Fall*.

Partial support for this project was provided by the Philbrick
family and by donations to the Philbrick Poetry Project Fund.

Generous funding was also provided by a grant from the Rhode
Island State Council on the Arts, through an appropriation by
the Rhode Island General Assembly and a grant from the
National Endowment for the Arts.

RISCA
Art is the Anchor

CONTENTS

For Julie

A BETTER WAY
TO FALL

... he made two pairs of wings for
them. They put them on and just before
they took flight Daedalus warned
Icarus to keep a middle course over the
sea. If he flew too high the sun might
melt the glue and the wings drop off.
However, as stories so often show,
what elders say youth disregards.

— Edith Hamilton, *Mythology*

Icarus

Fuck your cautionary tale.
I have ears, heard
his warning, knew
what I wanted. So? No
sob. No could've been.
Try this cliché for keeps:
not youth, but love —
Ariadne reading in my
father's study, her beauty
perfect, or so I thought
before I spent millennia
comparing. And him?
Big man? Theseus? I
tried sabotage. Went
to Minos, fawn-eyed,
ratted out their plans
to flee. I have no coin
for the ferry. It was eons
before I gave up trying
to hold on. Don't fly
too close: easy moral.
Tragic, true, but
a moment in the sun?
Eternal. What hell?
I never felt the fall.

Sgt. Bradley Talks Emergency Procedure

We come to when he says raise
all shades, when he says snipers
will take high ground, will be
our eyes, and when it starts,
he says, stay down, says
all hands on heads and single
file when you exit; it's
SOP, he says, too many
backpacks, and experience has taught us
they're innocent until the bullet's
in your chest. Here's the word
that means lock down. Here's the room
where you'll huddle. Here's the only knock
that means it's safe. Anticipate.
Drill. You think you won't,
but every study shows
you'll lose your head. I don't mean
to alarm, he says, but
three hours plus a day right now
those kids are playing games
that train a boy to squeeze off rounds
like this, this, this. And this is how
it happened in Moses Lake, and this
is what they did in Jonesboro, and this
is all you didn't want to know
of Columbine — the homemade fractals,
the detailed schematics. And you,
he says, are our best defense.

Paunch and bald patch, sag
and bad dye, we're cataloging long
coats and sullen stares, running
the percentages, calculating second-story
drops and the density of fire doors.
Our minds are buzzing television.
We can almost hear the story
spinning off the perpetual machine.

To a Former Student Training
To Be an Interrogator

They say pressure isn't torture
and, at times, because I don't know better
I'm willing to agree
as I'm willing to believe
they live to kill our people.
                I told you
just months ago, in literature,
unlike life, everything happens for a reason

as you struggled through Act III, scene iv, *Macbeth,*
our hero-villain shocked by a ghost of his own making,
and, again, again, I asked,
                      what does he mean?
. . .the worm that's fled
Hath nature that in time will venom breed,

                             and
. . .never shake / Thy gory locks at me.

After those photos (stacked bodies, dogs, electrodes, hoods)
and month by month the rumors of something darker
done in our name, I can't fathom your decision,

though I remember the affable grin
when the difficult text
clicked, and I can almost see your face
turned toward that shadowed other.

The War on Terror

July 2003

By the look of her we know
that every sense is razored
as her bare feet heel-toe heel-
toe it through the damp grass
in the night, the backyard
diffusing in a bank of fog
where a wet sheet struggles
to get off the line,
        and since good horror
sweet-talks empathy
into getting in the car, our eyes
widen their well mouths,
our blind hearts rise
to the bait of her voice,
the hairline fracture in her
timbre threatening to crack
each time she calls for Max,
whose guard-dog-bark-turned-
yelp, like a quick brake of tires,
rushed her out here
in a nightgown sheer and
clingy enough for us
to wince at such naked
vulnerability, the camera
panning out to testify
to the limits of her
jaundiced flashlight beam
in the face of so much darkness
that gets that much darker
as the flashlight stutters, and she,
shaking it, wobbles

on hysteria's tightrope just
long enough for us to
lean in that much more,
so glad we spent nine-fifty
and our Saturday night this way,
because, these days, it's a relief
to know what's next — the marquee
guaranteeing something ultra,
the director working hard
to fill his blood quota —
so we suck our teeth
as if what's coming,
like all inoculations,
burns, it pulling into focus
that what's jerking on the line
is what's becoming
of her dog / her mouth
rigid for the tight shot,
her scream percussive
in our chests, a shudder
in the fog revealing what
we fear, this anticipation
so familiar we reach
our hands for the hands
of those beside us
as a violin revs up
and up the scales, aching
for that note where it or us
or something onscreen
must snap.

Minotaur

I'd say it's just the bass that's hammering my brain,
the unknown hours I've been reeling towards the bar
each time my bottle comes up empty, but I swear
I've known a nightmare that begins this way: the walls
of writhing flesh, the fog that's slashed by blood-
red laser light, the acrid burn of sweat and smoke
in eyes leering at women slinking by. I try
to navigate this labyrinth of skin on skin
but sense my spool of memory is all spun out;
like the trail of smoke I exhale at every turn,
it's disappeared. Where are my friends? Where is the girl
I ditched them for? What do I call this shape that crawls
past me on all fours? Why won't these bodies whirling
faster finally fall? In my nightmare I get out
now. This is no nightmare. He's been watching me, waits:
horns lowered, shoulders hunched, the leather
    skull, the grin.

Redeemer

That Lent, most days, the plows
were out in force. Fridays, the nuns
would count heads, lead us — mittened,
booted, bent against the wind
like cowled penitents — in a single-file plod

across the yard from school to church
for stations of the cross. There,
in the half-gloom, thick with God's musk
of damp wool and wood polish,
again I'd rate my aching knees

against His agony, the stone reliefs
of that fish-bone body
shivering in the votives' light
as fourteen times we were impressed
with the meaning of this barter

of His torture for our sin: *thou hast
redeemed the world*. This was the winter
my father was arrested and the bomb
first corkscrewed through my dreams.
Nights before the protest, he tucked me in

with tales of biblical rebels: Shadrach,
Meshach, and Abednego, cucumber-cool
in the furnace blast; Daniel lounging
among charmed lions; St. Peter
sprung from Herod's cell to amble

past his jailors. Behind each happy ending,
an 11th hour angel towered, deadpan
and aerial as any caped crusader. Still
I'd lie awake, listening to all St. Catherine's
high stone arches echo *unto dust*

thou shalt return as they had that afternoon
I filed back to class and bus and home
across an earth moonscaped by snow
afraid to touch the ritual smudge
I wore like a dark third eye.

Etymology

The bomb will wait forever for its purpose.
Outside my room, she screeches, *It's the bomb!*

which means, *it's cool*
that men urge calm while earning ribbons
        riding bronco bomb.

Remember how we fretted that our taxes fed
        the bloated bomb?
How every movie starred that one sweat bead

that always almost fell
from the nose of the man with a key and his finger
        on the bomb?

Later we learned of the womb of the bomb,
how children of the bomb like spiders from an egg sack flew.

The projector whirs.
We hold our breath as the bomb from the hatch grows dim

then flowers.

The Trip to My Great Uncle's Wake

9/11/01

We packed the night before. Dark suits,
dark blue dress in dry clean plastic
on hangers in the back of the minivan.
Left in the dark. My father hates radio,
drove without talking. My mother and I,
sun up, rehashed gossip. It got old.
Avoided toll roads. Took I-86 East
past Jamestown, Binghamton. The trees
were on the edge of tourist season.
Had packed lunch: tuna fish, iced tea,
potato chips. Ate at a pull off's
wood shelter. Saw no one. The bathroom,
predictably, reeked. Years of brittle needles
beneath the picnic table. Nine hours.
The hypnotic run of telephone wires
that must have been singing.
My father pushed eighty. We were in a hurry.
The wake was at four. My mother
broke the silence, wondered
if my brother in Queens would beat us
to New Haven. Nothing I thought of
meant much. All day, the air, invisibly,
flooded. The satellites choked.
There wasn't a plane in the sky
anywhere in America. But you know that part.
Where were you? We were bored,
then glad, for a moment, we'd arrived.

Aneurysm

for P.L. 1974-2001

The resolution's so poor it takes a second
to adjust: not a weather vane, not
the chimney. Sixteen, he's on my roof

and then not. Cut by glare, his fall
smacks of every amateur disaster
pimped by Action News: the dizzying

focal drop, the shrieks from all of us
convinced the dare's gone south.
Even as the camera catches him

the moment he explodes the pool,
sends water-shrapnel beading up the lens,
and we erupt for his death defying,

what brought him down isn't evident,
but, so they tell us, there all the same.

Ariadne

Ten trillion fevered suns have drowned
    since on this island illness left me
        quarantined. In sweat-soaked dreams

I shriek the awful plummet down:
    the sun-kissed wings that hiss upon the sea,
        the body, a shell picked clean,

that gives in to the tidal toss and pull.
    Yes, I am Ariadne, princess become
        anchorite, virgin become a hero's whore,

who trembled for Theseus with a lust
    crueler than Poseidon's curse
        that drove my queen to fuck the bull

that made my half-brother horned
    and terrible. I made my choice,
        threatened Daedalus with lies, dangled

words like *traitor, torture, orphaned boy*
    until he yielded me the thread
        that pulled the nightmare body down.

And still you each come stumbling
    across the eons, feigning love but seeking
        wisdom, as if once more I knew the way,

as if each sunset were not Icarus,
    as if this myth had had its run
        and I were finally done with it.

Field Trip: Exhibit

How far it's come, epochs
and continents. Before man
deified the lightning's fire,

its tuba heart had clunked
from the cage of its body.

Before mother clasped infant,
on guard against the tall grass
transformed by night,

it shit great cairns, humped,
they think, some clumsy way.

Gathered round its bones
we sense that something's
changing in the air,

under those same stars
that now, like it, we've named.

Coming to Terms

Gatsby believed in the green light, the orgastic future
that year by year recedes before us.
                                    — F. Scott Fitzgerald

Tone, that nuanced-attitude-stew no recipe can catch,
is always hell to teach. *Fitzgerald here is reverent,*
but clearly pessimistic, less derisive than reflective,

less didactic than sincere. And even when I've slogged
hip deep through tonal vocab, sweating what I sense
but cannot name, there's always the trouble of palate,

your mom again surprised when I tear up from the garlic
in her hummus: *What, too much?* Who's to say, exactly,
why one's *gloomy* is another's *comic irony*? Even so,

I always trusted symbols, those concrete objects
representing clear ideas a class could memorize
and I could safely test: the <u>green</u> light on Daisy's dock,

evening, late spring, the end of Chapter One. I knew
they knew how it worked: the crucifix, the stoplight,
the flag. Then came news of your second tour

in a desert country, and today, mid-class, I'm telling them
about Camp Webster, how you and I, just twelve,
were goofing as the P.A. blasted reveille when all at once

Chuck Shipley's dad was in our faces screaming,
"Do you know what it's like to see your best friend
shot? Do you know what that flag means?"

Of course we didn't. Or did, but didn't. We'd never heard
of Korea, couldn't know Old Glory like this paunchy,
average father. And this morning, looking at those kids,

I knew why he believed we'd never see it his way.
That, at least, is what I told my juniors
before writing on the board that Gatsby's light

stands for *loss* as much as *hope*, that sometimes
it's a particle and sometimes a wave.

Google Earth

At first, the planet, then our landmass
    sculpted by eroding oceans. The jut
        of Florida. The sensuous Californian curve.

Imagine the warm Gulf waters lap.
    Scan the palm-wide bread basket.
        You can't help but see the demarcations

that are not there, those gold-star stickers
    over forty-eight capitals
        that conjure a pantheon

of landlocked constellations:
    The Pale Blue Ox, The Cherry Tree,
    Crockett's Cradled Gun.

To type in your address, one
    in over one hundred million,
        is to plummet past those mountains' majesty

until a grid and then discernible buildings
    emerge from the pixilated mist,
        the cockpit's nosedive suddenly hovering

just short of impact and static.
    The roof above is now below your eye.
    The pine tree weighed by snow

is bare. And that's your car,
    or was. Like an unearthed family photo,
        exactly when the shot was taken

puzzles. It was a bright day, spring
by the dogwood's bloom.
Go outside.

Shiver in the March wind:
black night, new moon, a satellite
blinking as it passes overhead.

When It's Her Turn

she tells me what to do with her body.
They say parenthood means we must do this
and get it on paper, and have it notarized
and maybe a lawyer should be involved.
We're looking into it. She breezes through

life support, DNR, feeding tubes, stresses
that they should take anything useful —
Even eyes? Even eyes. — and sew her shut.
Her flannel pajamas are crazy with tiny umbrellas.
I picture sutures beneath them, running up

like a zipper, teeth caught on the skin
between her breasts. I confess, it was her body
in a bar that drew me to this breakfast nook,
the mortgage that has us underwater, the baby
daughter who swam inside her, whose skin,

they've told us, insists on her touch.
That she doesn't want a church, she admits,
will be a bone in the throat of the family.
Not for her mother, maybe, but her father.
She asks that I care for her here, wants

sufficient medication for pain. Her words
are an ax behind glass, the water we've stashed
for disaster. I picture myself with her body
in a strange room without her. Ashes, she says,
and people should pray if they want to.

Daedalus

Barely older than you will always be,
I vowed to honor her till death.
Should I have known, those months

we swelled with hope, that Atropos
was set to cut a life, even as her sister
spun you yours? My son,

I let the wet nurse be your family,
ground my teeth each time your cry
caught me inking out the fates

of hundreds in the web of my design.
The candle drips as I retrace
my steps. Like memory, it must

consume itself before it can go dark.
For thirty years your falling cry
has thread its accusation deeper:

There is no killer but your father.
Icarus, mercy. At last, tonight,
navigate escape for me.

ABOUT THE POET

After earning his M.F.A. from Ohio State University, David O'Connell taught high school English for nearly a decade. His poems have been published in *Columbia Poetry Review, Drunken Boat, Poet Lore,* and *Rattle*, among other journals. He has received two fellowships from the Rhode Island State Council on the Arts.

ACKNOWLEDGEMENTS

Grateful acknowledgement is made to the editors of the following journals for publishing these poems, sometimes in earlier forms:

Boxcar Poetry Review: "Redeemer"
Bryant Literary Review: "To a Former Student Training to Be an Interrogator"
Columbia Poetry Review: "When It's Her Turn"
Fugue: "Minotaur"
Fickle Muses: "Ariadne," "Daedalus," and "Icarus"
Solstice: "Field Trip: Exhibit" (as "Exhibit")
Unsplendid: "Aneurysm"
Verse Online: "Sgt. Bradley Talks Emergency Procedure"

I would also like to thank the Rhode Island State Council on the Arts for the fellowships that supported the writing of this book.

This book was typeset by The Poet's Press for The Providence Athenaeum in Calisto type with ITC Symbol and Futura titles. Two hundred copies were printed, of which 26 are signed and lettered by the author.

This is the fifteenth title in the Philbrick Poetry Project chapbook series. The previous titles are:

Coats Field by Marjorie Milligan (1999)
The Singed Horizon by Mimi White (2000)
Percussion, Salt & Honey by Nehassaiu deGannes (2001)
What We Planted by Laura Cherry (2002)
AntiGraphi by Linda Voris (2003)
Mr. Gravity's Blue Holiday by Justin Lacour (2004)
Heady Rubbish by Lynn Tudor Deming (2005)
Last Summer by J. F. Connolly (2006)
Toward Anguish by Leslie McGrath (2007)
Chrysalis by John Brush (2008)
Auction by Jennifer E. Whitten (2009)
The Waiting Room by Kathleen M. Kelley (2010)
Workers' Rites by Ellen LaFleche (2011)
Neither Created Nor Destroyed by Lucille Burt (2012)

Made in the USA
Charleston, SC
13 April 2013